# A to Z Mexico

## BY JUSTINE AND RON FONTES

children's press®

A Division of Scholastic Inc.
New York  Toronto  London  Auckland  Sydney
Mexico City  New Delhi  Hong Kong
Danbury, Connecticut

Series Consultant: Linda D. Bullock, Ph.D.
Series Design: Marie O'Neill
Book Design: Symon Chow
Photo Research: Candlepants Incorporated

The photos on the cover show an Iguana (top), a sculpture in the Western Plaza of Copan (right), a Tarahumara girl (bottom), and red chilies (left).

Photographs ©2003: Corbis Images: 28 bottom (AFP), 15 top (Albright-Knox Art Gallery), cover right, 13 top (Archivo Iconografico, S.A.), 36 (Morton Beebe), 12 top, 14, 33 (Bettmann), 28 top (Steve Chenn), 15 bottom (Christie's Images), 13 bottom (Richard A. Cooke), 37 bottom (Richard Cummins), 10 bottom (Keith Dannemiller), 27 left, 31 bottom, 38 right (Macduff Everton), cover left, 7 (Randy Faris), cover bottom (Natalie Fobes), 24 bottom (Gerald French), 23 (Dan Guravich), 11 left (Robert Holmes), 32 (Hulton-Deutsch Collection), 35 left (Bob Krist), 6 bottom, 9 top right, 9 bottom, 29, 37 top right (Danny Lehman), 4 left, 5 bottom, 16 bottom, 38 left (Charles and Josette Lenars), 25 bottom (Charles O'Rear), 35 right (Gianni Dagli Orti), 27 right (Carl & Ann Purcell), 34 (Kevin Schafer), 10 top, 16 top (Phil Schermeister), 30 (ML Sinibaldi), 26 (James A. Sugar), 5 right (Kennan Ward), 17 top (Nik Wheeler), 31 top (Peter M. Wilson), 6 top (Michael S. Yamashita), 18; Corbis SABA/Keith Dannemiller: 9 top left; Corbis Sygma/Pizzoli Alberto: 12 bottom; Getty Images: cover top (G.K. & Vikki Hart), 11 right (Louis B. Wallach), 4 right, 5 left; ImageState: 8 top, 22; MapQuest.com, Inc.: 21; PhotoDisc/Getty Images: 24 top right, 25 top left (Sexto Sol), 24 top left (Don Tremain); PictureQuest: 17 bottom (Joe Atlas/Brand X Pictures), 19 bottom (Burke/Triolo), 8 bottom (Philip Coblentz), 37 top left (Creatas); The Image Bank/Getty Images/Guido/Alberto Rossi: 25 top right; The Image Works/Cameramann: 19 top.
Map by XNR Productions

Library of Congress Cataloging-in-Publication Data

Fontes, Justine.
  Mexico / by Justine and Ron Fontes.– 1st American ed.
    p. cm. – (A to Z)
Contents: Animals – Buildings – Cities – Dress – Exports – Food – Government – History – Important people – Jobs – Keepsakes – Land – Map – Nation – Only in Mexico – People – Question – Religion – School and sports – Transportation – Unusual places – Visiting the country – Window to the past – X-tra special things – Yearly festivals – Zapatos – Let's explore more.
  ISBN 0-516-24565-1 (lib. bdg.)          0-516-26815-5 (pbk.)
  1.  Mexico–Juvenile literature. [1. Mexico.]  I. Fontes, Ron. II. Title. III. Series.
  F1208.5.K67 2003
  972–dc21

                                2003003700

1 2 3 4 5 6 7 8 9 10 R 12 11 10 09 08 07 06 05 04 03

# Contents

Iguana

# Animals

## Coyote

*(kye-OH-tee)*
is spelled the
same in English
and Spanish.

Coyotes, rabbits, deer, and snakes live
throughout Mexico. Alligators and
tarantulas live in the rain forests.
Jaguars do, too.

Tarantula

Jaguar

Jaguars are big cats. They pounce on their prey from tree branches where they rest. Jaguars are good swimmers. They use their front paws to flip fish out of the water. Sometimes they attack alligators!

A tarantula's hairy legs help these big spiders hunt at night. They can feel their prey move in the dark.

There are about 700 **species**, or kinds, of iguanas in Mexico. Some grow to be more than six feet long.

**Jaguars are often seen in Mexican art.**

# Buildings

**The Palace of Fine Arts has balconies and archways.**

The Olmec people lived in Mexico from 1200 to 400 B.C. They built the first American pyramid from dirt and rocks.

The Maya lived in Mexico from 250 B.C. to A.D. 900. They built pyramids from stone. Later, the Aztecs came to Mexico. They also built pyramids.

The Spanish came to Mexico in 1519 and ruled Mexico for 300 years. Some of their buildings had **balconies** and archways. Some were made from adobe, a brick made from mud and straw. Adobe walls keep buildings cool in the summer and warm in the winter.

# Cities

Mexico City is one of the biggest cities in the world. Nearly 22 million people live there. Only Tokyo, Japan, has more people.

Many Mexican cities have a central plaza with statues, fountains, and a park. Churches, government buildings, movie theaters, and markets are often near the plaza.

Mexico City sits in a bowl-shaped valley that traps smoke from factories and cars. The city's air is the most polluted in the world. On windless days, people can barely see across the street, and schools are closed.

Native dancers wearing traditional clothing

# Dress

*Serapes*

People who live in small villages often wear clothes like those of their **ancestors**. City people usually wear modern clothes.

This man is wrapped in a *serape*. *Serapes* are blankets worn over the shoulders.

# Sombra

*(SOAM-brah)*
means shade.
The word sombrero
(soam-BREH-roh)
comes from sombra.

Many Mexican women wear brightly decorated clothes. Some wear **rebozos**, or shawls, that cover the head.

In sunny parts of Mexico, men often wear plain white cotton shirts and pants. Wide-brimmed felt or straw *sombreros* shade their eyes. Sombreros are hats.

Each region of Mexico has its own special designs for colorful, handmade cloth. The cloth is used to make *ponchos* and **serapes**.

Many skilled people turn raw silver like this into beautiful jewelry, candlesticks, and other items for export.

**Oil rig**

# Exports

Mexico trades most with the United States. Oil is one of Mexico's leading **exports**. Mexico is the sixth largest producer of oil.

Mexico also exports machinery, chemicals, cotton, and food. The biggest export crop is corn. Other crops are wheat, tomatoes, rice, coffee, vanilla, and *cacao*, or chocolate.

Mexico produces more silver than any other country in the world.

## Mexican Guacamole Recipe

**WHAT YOU NEED:**
- 2 ripe avocados, pitted, peeled, and chopped
- 1/2 onion, finely chopped
- 1 tomato, finely chopped
- 2 green chili peppers, finely chopped
- 1 tbsp. lemon juice
- ground cumin, chili powder, pepper, and salt

**HOW TO MAKE IT:**
Mash the avocados. Mix in the onion, tomato, peppers, and lemon juice. Add spices to taste.

*Tortillas*

# Food

Two popular foods in Mexico are beans and **tortillas**, or flat cakes made from cornmeal or flour. Mexicans often use tortillas to scoop up food.

Another tasty Mexican food is **guacamole**. Ask an adult to help you make some, using the recipe above.

Benito Juárez

# Government

**Today, Vicente Fox Quesada is the president of Mexico.**

All Mexicans 18 years or older can vote. They vote for the people who will speak for them in Congress, including the president. Mexico has a president but no vice-president. Mexico's presidents are elected to six-year terms and cannot run again.

Benito Juárez was a great Mexican president. His parents died when he was only three. Benito was poor but found ways to go to school to become a lawyer. He was elected president in 1861 and passed laws to help poor people.

# History

**Hernán Cortés**

The Maya are one of the many different people who have ruled Mexico. They built huge buildings decorated with sculptures and invented a system of writing and the calendar we use today.

Then came the Aztecs. The Aztecs were also great builders. They fought many wars with their neighbors. The Aztecs made their prisoners work as slaves.

The Aztecs had never seen ships, horses, or pale-skinned people before Hernán Cortés came. He was a Spanish explorer. Cortés defeated the Aztecs in 1521. Spain ruled Mexico for the next 300 years.

**Mayan ruins**

Diego Rivera and Frida Kahlo

# Important People

Diego Rivera and Frida Kahlo are famous Mexican artists. Their colorful paintings are known all over the world.

*Self Portrait with Monkey,*
by **Frida Kahlo**, 1938

# Pintor

*(peen-tor)*
means
painter.

Diego painted large wall paintings called **murals**. His most famous mural is on a wall of the National Palace in Mexico City. Diego died in 1957.

When Frida was 15, she was in a horrible bus accident. Afterward, Frida taught herself to paint. She met Diego while he was painting a mural in her school auditorium. They were married in 1929. Frida died in 1954.

*Girl of Tehuantepec,*
by **Diego Rivera**, 1936

# Jobs

Many Mexican people are poor. Most of these people live in cities, where they work for low pay in stores, restaurants, and factories. Others work as fishers and wood-cutters. Some Mexicans work on farms or ranches.

In southern Mexico, farmers grow many different crops on small farms. In northern Mexico, ranchers raise cattle. Ranchers on Mexico's dry **plateau** raise sheep. In the mountains, they raise goats.

**Many Mexican children work to help their families.**

**Fisherman**

## Pescador

*(PESS-kah-dor)* is a fisherman.

These shells once belonged to large sea snails called conches.

# Keepsakes

Many sombreros are made of straw. This fancy hat is red velvet.

Mexico has almost 6,000 miles (9,600 km) of beaches. People from all over the world come to enjoy them. A conch shell is a nice way to remember Mexico's warm sand, blue water, and sunny skies.

You can find many things to buy in Mexico's open-air markets. People gather in city plazas to sell sombreros, pottery, **embroidered** clothes, and silver jewelry. They also sell fresh fruits and vegetables, warm tortillas, and other tasty foods. **Mariachis** stroll the plazas, playing and singing.

# Land

Some of Mexico's tallest mountains are volcanoes. Volcanoes form when melted rock works its way through Earth's crust and spills or bursts onto the land.

**Prickly pear cactus and other cacti are grown for food in Mexico. People peel off the spines before they eat them.**

Mexico also has several mountain ranges. Two are the Sierra Madre Occidental and the Sierra Madre Oriental. These ranges run up and down Mexico's west and east coasts.

In northern Mexico, there are deserts. Special kinds of plants called cacti grow in the desert. Most cacti have prickly spines. Some have beautiful flowers. Cacti do not need much water to live.

## Sierra
(see-EHRR-ah)
means a
mountain range.

**Popocatépetl (poh-poh-kaw-TAY-peh-tuhl) is a volcano near Puebla, Mexico.**

19

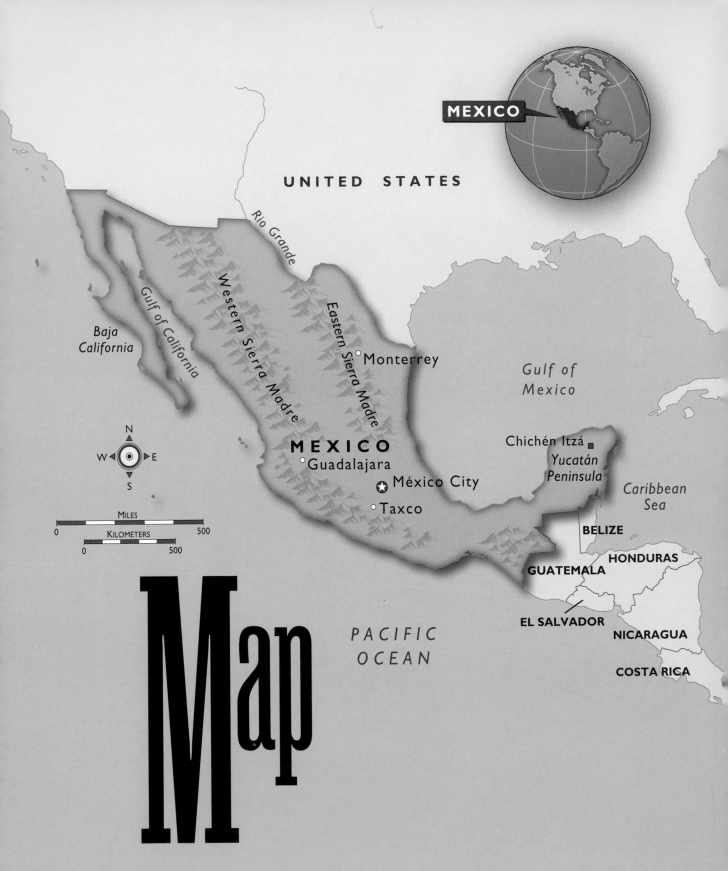

MEXICO

UNITED STATES

Rio Grande

Baja
California

Gulf of California

Western Sierra Madre

Eastern Sierra Madre

Monterrey

Gulf of
Mexico

N
W E
S

MEXICO

Guadalajara

México City

Taxco

Chichén Itzá

Yucatán
Peninsula

Caribbean
Sea

MILES
0          500

KILOMETERS
0          500

BELIZE

HONDURAS

GUATEMALA

EL SALVADOR

NICARAGUA

COSTA RICA

PACIFIC
OCEAN

Map

# Nation

## Bandera

*(BAN-dehrr-ah)*
is a flag or
banner.

The Mexican flag is green, white, and red. The green stands for hope. White stands for unity and honesty. Red stands for the blood of Mexico's heroes.

The flag shows an **emblem** that comes from an Aztec **legend**. The legend says that a god of war told the Aztec people to build a city where they saw an eagle sitting on a prickly-pear cactus and eating a snake. The Aztecs built a great city called Tenochtitlán (tay-nok-TEE-tlahn). Today, Mexico City sits where Tenochtitlán once stood.

Costumed dancers doing
the Mexican Hat Dance

# Only in Mexico

The Mexican Hat Dance is the national dance of Mexico. It is one of many folk dances performed at *fiestas*, or celebrations.

# Bailar

*(BAH-ee-lahr)*
means to dance.
It comes from
the Latin word,
ballare.

**Monarch butterflies**

In the fall, monarch butterflies fly up to 2,000 miles (3,200 km) to Mexico. Traveling many miles per day, the monarchs rest in Mexico's forests until spring. Then they fly home again. On warm days, millions of butterflies leave the trees and fly through the Mexican sky.

Monarch butterflies help make Mexico colorful. So do Mexico's music, dance, and costumes, which are as bright as butterfly wings!

Close families are the
heart of Mexican life.
The head of the family
is often the grandfather
or great-grandfather.

# People

Some Mexican people have Indian ancestors.
Some have ancestors from Europe, especially
Spain. Most Mexicans have both.

# Ciudad

*(SEE-oo-dahd)*
means city.

Families spend much time together. They celebrate family occasions and holidays, such as the Day of the Dead. On this day, families remember their ancestors.

Mexicans live in all kinds of homes. Some are older style adobe homes, like the photo in the center. Inside these homes, families gather to share big meals. Family life is very important to Mexican people. Most children live at home until they get married.

# Question

## Did Mexican Indians invent basketball?

Many tribes of Mexican Indians played ball games. One game was called *Tlachtli*. Some people say this game was the beginning of basketball.

Tlachtli was played on a court. A stone or wooden ring hung over the middle of the court. Players used their legs, hips, and elbows to move a hard ball and put it through the ring.

Playing ball in ancient times was often dangerous. Losers were killed on the court where they played. Aren't you glad basketball has changed?

The Metropolitan Cathedral is found in Mexico City.

# Religion

Most Mexicans are Roman Catholics and go to church often. Mexico's oldest and largest church is in Mexico City. This grand church is called the Metropolitan Cathedral.

The Spanish brought the Roman Catholic faith to Mexican Indians in the 1500s. Today, Catholic beliefs and ancient Indian beliefs are mixed together.

Almost every town and village in Mexico has a church and a **patron saint**. The Virgin of Guadalupe is the patron saint of all of Mexico. People hold fiestas on December 12 to honor her.

# School & Sports

The **Mexican Revolution** changed the lives of schoolchildren. After the revolution, all Mexican children could go to free public schools. Before the revolution, few of Mexico's people could read and write.

Soccer is the most popular sport in Mexico. Even children in tiny villages play. They use tall cacti as goal posts. Children and adults spend many hours learning to play soccer.

# Transportation

Mexico's largest airport is in Mexico City. Once visitors arrive, they move through the city in cars, trucks, buses, and on motorcycles. All of this traffic creates pollution.

Mexico City opened its subway system in 1969. Today, this system of underground trains has eleven lines that carry people under the city. All together, the subway is more than 120 miles (200 km) long. It is one of the cheapest subways in the world.

Trains, cars, and airplanes also carry people and goods across Mexico.

# Unusual Places

There are underground rivers in the Yucatán **peninsula**. In some places, the rivers have hollowed out big caverns, or caves. Sometimes a cavern's roof falls in. The result is a **cenote**, or natural well.

The Maya carved pictures on rocks inside cenotes to show their **ceremonies**. Some cenotes are filled with the bones of people killed to please the Maya's water god. Scientists have also found valuable objects in cenotes. Brave people go scuba diving in cenotes and water-filled caves.

There are four stairways on this pyramid. It has 365 steps.

# Visiting the Country

The Aztecs built floating gardens like those that grow today near Mexico City. They built the gardens on **chinampas**, or rafts, that could be moved from the sun to the shade. Aztecs used boats to carry their crops to market. Today, people can ride boats through these floating gardens.

Hundreds of people once lived in the ancient Maya city of Chichén Itzá. The pyramids there still stand today.

# Window to the Past

Dance has deep roots in Mexico. Maya, Aztecs, and other native people danced to talk to their gods. The teenagers above perform the Dance of the Little Old Men.

This boy is boiling tree sap to make chewing gum. The sap must be stirred for three to six hours.

Some Mexicans still make chewing gum the old-fashioned way. They cut the bark of **sapodilla** trees to collect the **chicle**, or gooey sap, that leaks from the cuts. The sap is boiled and mixed with sugar and flavors to make chewing gum.

Mexicans have kept their past alive with songs, dances, and traditional ways of doing things.

Olmec sculpture

# X-tra Special Things

**Aztec calendar**

You can see Mexico's history through the amazing things left by its ancestors. The Olmec built awesome stone statues with huge carved heads.

Both the Maya and the Aztecs had 365-day calendars like our own. In the center of the calendar above is the Aztec sun god.

In this picture above left, four daring *voladores,* or fliers, are doing an ancient dance, they jump from a tall pole and swing round and round the pole. A fifth person on the top of the pole plays a flute or drums as the fliers swirl down to the ground.

# Yearly Festivals

Mexicans celebrate many holidays. Some are meant to remember family and loved ones. Others recall events from history.

**The Day of the Dead**

**Piñatas are balloons filled with candy and toys. Children wear blindfolds and take turns trying to break the piñata with a stick.**

At midnight on September 15, church bells ring and fireworks explode. These mark the beginning of Mexican Independence Day. September 16 is a holiday all over Mexico, with singing, dancing, and great food.

On November 1 and 2, people celebrate the Day of the Dead. Children wear costumes and collect candy. Mexican families also bring candles and spend the night at the graves of their loved ones.

37

**In some parts of Mexico, tiny charms are called *milagros*. *Milagros* decorate this shoe.**

# Zapatos

Mexicans wear all kinds of *zapatos,* or shoes. Plain *huaraches*, or sandals, are often worn every day in warm weather.

Some shoes are worn to do special things. Dancers who dance traditional dances wear special slippers and boots. Athletes, such as soccer players, wear sports shoes.

## Spanish and English Words

**ancestor** (AN-sess-tur) a family member who lived long ago

**balcony** (BAL-kuh-nee) a platform that has railings and sits on the outside of a building

**cenote** (si-NOH-tee) a natural well

**ceremony** (SER-uh-moh-nee) an action, word, and often music performed to mark an important occasion, like a wedding

**chicle** (CHI-klay) the gooey sap of the *sapodilla* tree which is used to make chewing gum

**chinampas** (chee-NAM-pahs) floating gardens originally made by the *Aztecs*; the gardens were built on rafts so that they could be moved from one place to another

**coyote** (kye-OH-tee) an animal that looks like a small wolf, or dog and lives in the western United States

**emblem** (EM-bluhm) a symbol or a sign

**embroidered** (em-BROI-durd) that has a picture or design sewn onto it

**export** (EK-sport) a product sold by one country to another

**fiestas** (fee-ESS-tuhs) Spanish word for celebrations

**guacamole** (gwah-kuh-MOH-leh) a dip made of avocado, tomatoes, onions, and seasonings

**legend** (LEJ-uhnd) a story handed down from long ago; although legends are usually based on facts, they are not completely true

**mariachi** (mah-ree-AH-chee) a type of music that is popular in the state of Jalisco, in Mexico

**Mexican Revolution** (MEK-si-kuhn rev-uh-LOO-shuhn) the war that began in 1910 and freed Mexico from president Porfirio Díaz, a dictator who had ruled the country by force for over 30 years

**milagros** (MEE-lah-grohs) tiny charms; also the Spanish word for miracles

**mural** (MYU-ruhl) a painting on a wall

**patron saint** (PAY-truhn SAYNT) a saint that looks after a particular country or group of people

**peninsula** (puh-NIN-suh-luh) a piece of land that sticks out from a larger landmass and is almost completely surrounded by water

**plateau** (pla-TOH) an area of high, flat land

**rebozos** (reh-BOH-soss) Spanish word for wraps, shawls, or cloaks

**sapodilla** (sah-poh-DEE-yah) an evergreen tree made out of hard reddish wood that oozes a gooey sap called *chicle*, and yields a rough skinned brown fruit

**sculpture** (SKUHLP-chur) something that is shaped out of stone, wood, metal, or other materials.

**serapes** (seh-RAH-pehs) Spanish word for bright, colorful shawls that men wear over their shoulders, especially in Mexico

**species** (SPEE-sees) a group of animals or plants of the same kind that can mate and have offspring.

**tortillas** (tor-TEE-yuhs) a round, flat bread made from cornmeal or flour

## Let's Explore More

**Fiesta Femenina Celebrating Women in Mexican Folktales** retold by Mary-Joan Gerson, Barefoot Books, 2001

**The Aztecs Facts Stories Activities** by Robert Nicholson and Claire Watts, Chelsea House Publishers, 1994

**The Maya** by Jacqueline Dembar Greene, Franklin Watts ,1992

## Websites

**www.mexican-embassy.dk/history.html**
Learn about the history and culture of Mexico on this site.

**http://www.elbalero.gob.mx/index_kids.html**
This site includes information on Mexican culture, government, news, games, pictures to color, and other fun activities.

# Index

*Italic* page numbers indicate illustrations.

# Meet the Authors

**JUSTINE & RON FONTES** have written nearly 400 children's books together. Since 1988, they have published *critter news*, a free newsletter that keeps them in touch with publishers from their home in Maine.

The Fonteses have written many biographies and early readers, as well as historical novels and other books combining facts with stories. Their love of animals is expressed in the nature notes columns of *critter news*.

During his childhood in Tennessee, Ron was a member of the Junior Classical League and went on to tutor Latin students. At 16, Ron was drawing a science fiction comic strip for the local newspaper. A professional artist for 30 years, Ron has also been in theater as a costumer, makeup artist, and designer.

Justine was born in New York City and worked in publishing while earning a BA in English Literature Phi Beta Kappa from New York University. Thanks to her parents' love of travel, Justine visited most of Europe as a child, going as far north as Finland. During college, she spent time in France and Spain.